Dodging the Illusion: Agent, Beware

By Q.O.W.

DODGING THE ILLUSION: AGENT BEWARE

First edition. January 7, 2026.

ISBN: 979-8232380489

Written by Q.O.W.

Acknowledgement

To the Creator, known by many names, who grants us all the chance to co-create — this journey, though sometimes painful, has been deeply enlightening. Thank you for the mission.

Introduction

I composed this brief document as a tribute to the sacrificial — the people who have been sacrificed to systems that promise stability while instigating business models that destabilize the bottom of the proverbial "human pyramid" of service work. If you have been burned by an insurance-related employer, please know that it was not all in your head, but rather a premeditated plan to grift your energy, time, and materials.

To the new "captive" agent: you are just as important as the one who learned their lessons the hard way. You are the future of the sales industry. My hope is that, after you finish reading this, you will be awakened to this game of life — or life insurance (and all other lines) — as well as how to play it.

Since that is a mouthful to interpret, let me put it this way. Your desire to start an insurance career for flexibility, earning potential, and work-life balance is a noble one. The challenge lies not in having a vision, but in overcoming the negative influences that come with insurance business models promising wealth and financial independence while delivering little to no income stability. Illusions are often created by deceptive forces, which mislead both the inexperienced and the experienced. If not careful, the agent may find himself on the slippery slope of hindered success.

Fewer agents than you think can transparently describe how they navigated the challenges to successfully reach the apex of their careers. Several will admit that they tried the work of selling insurance — life, health, retirement, and/or auto and home — and decided the work just wasn't for them. Both groups were possibly predisposed to help individuals and communities. So what's the difference? Only you can answer that question.

My scope is to reveal the business models of four organizations. I hope this will provide insight into the cost of doing business as an insurance agent, broker, and/or sacrificial lamb.

Before we proceed, it is only fair to share a little about myself. I was wired to be bi-vocational. Educating others about insurance started off as a side hustle 15 years ago. Due to a changing economy and layoffs from my industry of choice, also in the financial sector, I entered the insurance field full time in 2022. Within three years of exploring different models and talking to more seasoned agents — compared with my own experience — I believe it is safe to say that the industry needs transformation.

Change will not come from the masters of illusion scattered across the agent universe. It will come from the ground up, from the base of the pyramid. You are the ones who make the money for everyone else. I hope to provide you with food for thought when deciding about partnering with the right opportunity and company model.

No one ever taught me the art of dodging the illusion of recruiting agents and savvy organizations. But now that I know, I will pass it on. The first step is to spread the word...

Scenario 1: the Illusion Weaver

Until you make the unconscious conscious, it will direct your life and you will call it fate. – Carl Jung

An "Illusion Weaver" evokes the idea of someone who can weave or create illusions — like a magical craftsman of perception.

My first full-time experience selling life insurance was a bittersweet journey into the upside-down world. The company had been recruiting me over a period of 10 years — more aggressively within a four-year period after the firm was refreshed with new partners. Since I was bi-vocational, I was never tempted to leave the stability of my 9-to-5.

Recruiters know that their targets eventually face changes in life and career. They email prospects repeatedly until they see an opening to go in for the kill. No pun intended — of course, a good recruiter knows its prey. I cannot hate the player, but I have learned to detest the game.

Finally, the right carrot was dangled before me, and I was snagged like a fish on a hook. The offer was a part-time opportunity that included an educational track to an insurance designation. What better temptation than to dream of running a firm one day? Having the proper letters behind one's name seemed like a good start. Insurance designations present the image of an experienced, trained agent that people can trust.

Another reason I was finally recruited: I simply hated my career. While navigating the sludge of working in Corporate America, I could not resist the temptation of investing in an enterprise that claimed it could provide me with more money and, eventually, more control of my time.

The expected sales goals did not seem too outrageous, so I strongly considered the offer — re-wrapped and presented to me at the perfect time, in the right environment, during a dead-end career. Things were getting worse, thanks to my industry tanking under rising interest rates and fly-by-night CEOs offering little security for financial analysts tied to struggling companies.

Perhaps a more entrepreneurial opportunity would be the better fit. Sales compensation was advertised as 100% commission plus bonuses, and the agent was incentivized to reach out to his or her own natural market.

A natural market entails the people within your own circle of influence. In other words, you are expected to ask your friends and family to buy insurance so that you can stay afloat during the first few months to a year. They neglected to tell us about the risk of family tensions and lost friends due to underwriting — and people who care about us too much to say no.

Some people stopped answering their phones when my number popped up, and some have not returned — even to this day. If you don't have a strong natural market, things will get really complicated, really fast.

◊ Reality Spark

I have found that the part-time option is often offered to hook the potential agent into signing a preliminary contract — eventually moving them toward a more permanent agreement. This provides the illusion of bonuses and mentorship while tapping, as quickly as possible, into the agent's personal network of family and friends. If the agent decides to leave prematurely, their potential contacts are left in the system as future leads for the chosen agents who are encouraged to stay with the firm.

I joined the organization with all the necessary licensing in place, which made me highly valuable — the company didn't need to invest in my credentials.

Retirement is a different story. In my scenario, I was able to pass my preliminary retirement licensing, which was sponsored by the company. In my opinion, this is the only reason to stay in contract — if you plan to have a long-term career in investment advising.

The exams are not as easy as the life insurance exam, and there will be much competition on your team to secure retirement-related clients. Since most companies do not offer leads, if you do not have your own network of viable clients — agent, beware.

My illusion weaver did not mention the above facts, only that the "real money" is made once you are credentialed as a "registered representative" with FINRA. Of course, you will need to meet sales goals while studying, undergoing state testing, and satisfying internal requirements.

Aside from the goals, you will need income — so selling is a must. One option is to work with a mentor agent on your team to set up appointments for retirement rollovers. That agent will get a percentage for helping you with the application, but you will have to find the prospects and set up the meetings.

The mentoring agents make money for showing up and submitting the application. In my three years, I have run into very few mentoring agents who said anything different in the meeting than I would have said myself. The prospect was either someone familiar or already "warmed up" because I had established a preliminary relationship during prospecting.

The new agent is responsible for almost all the "warming" of the clients-to-be. The mentoring agent is working to meet their own goals, and you are not their priority. However, you are the vital life force that keeps other agents alive in the game of insurance.

If it's in the back of your mind that you'll one day become a mentoring agent, believe that you will be at the mercy of leadership—and the competition to please that leader within your team. Good luck, because many of us can attest that partner-agent boundaries often blur in these scenarios. I asked too many questions, so I felt I was never allowed into the inner circle. After speaking with seasoned agents who either left or were pushed out of the firm, I learned that your recruiter is never meant to be your mentor—but rather the company's handler.

I can't say this applies to every organization, but in these models, there's often a trace of quid pro quo—because insurance sales is a transactional science. Sabotaging deals is difficult to prove and can lead to paranoia. However, if you lead with your intuition, you'll know when something feels off. I'm referring to the agent who's doing everything right—setting appointments, staying consistent, hitting five or more meetings a week. If this effort happened in a vacuum, free from the toxicity of narcissistic firm leaders, it might actually work—regardless of the product being sold.

However, the illusion weaver has crafted a prosperity narrative for his entire team and must secure their loyalty by providing them with a steady stream of income — even if it's off your back. He enjoys the rewards from the organization through bonuses for recruiting and pushing agents to close sales, while you're left with only the crumbs that fall from his table. It doesn't matter who you are — if you're not generating revenue for the organization, you're expendable. The illusion that hard work will lead to financial progression fades quickly.

It's rarely disclosed that your future will depend heavily on your assigned leader. And if you offend their ego — especially one that is bruised, vindictive, or even psychopathic — God help you all.

In these not-so-positive scenarios, your team will have a core inner circle of faithful sycophants willing to sell you out to keep their position and income. If you miss the red flags, they'll catch up to you — especially when your sales numbers start falling month after month. Not because you're a bad agent, but because you let them get into your head.

Now, what is the real reality of the business?

Depending on the company model, you may close business — and underwriting can still reverse the issued policy if the insured carries too much risk for the company. If the reversal happens at a certain point, you either won't get paid or will get hit with a negative debit on your register.

It'll make sense during training, but the real red flag is how the company manages your commissions. In some cases (as in Scenario 1), you'll have a register of both positive and negative transactions. The company may include overhead — such as printing, office space, or rental costs — in that register, right alongside your commissions.

Bonuses are calculated from sales goals minus any reversals due to customer cancellations or underwriting declines.

I left voluntarily with an $800 deficit. There were agents — even former "Agent of the Year" recipients — who had thousands in deficit on their registers. It's a risk they were willing to carry, so ask yourself honestly if you're prepared to survive the first couple of years living in the red.

I would call it indentured servitude, but the choice to take on that risk is up to you. If you ask about this during your interview, you'll be told: "It's always the agent, not the system." The company's modus operandi is to keep agents selling by running a tab.

Termination for not meeting sales goals is something agents never imagine they'll face. The goals seem reasonable during the interview. Typically, the evaluation period is three months.

In this company, I was on the chopping block for termination twice. I survived by selling in a frenzy — only to have those sales reversed the following month. Normally, your friends and family market is exhausted in a year. For me, it was closer to six months.

If the leadership likes you, they'll help — but only by providing the cold leads no one else could close. Good leads go to the chosen few who put loyalty above everything else, including common sense.

They'll pretend to reach out to leadership higher on the pyramid to advocate for you, but it's a performance. I turned things around because I was wired to persevere — but at a serious cost to my well-being. It didn't hurt them to keep me around, I suppose, because I had already communicated through my actions that my worth was cheap and easy to manipulate.

Many agents fall into this trap. They go off the radar by taking second jobs while keeping their insurance contract in place. The firm hopes they'll find new prospects through these jobs — a "win-win" for everyone except the agent, now juggling two roles.

In business models like this, agents are considered captive — meaning they can only sell for the organization. Other business activity typically must be disclosed, especially if the agent is registered with FINRA.

Some agents don't get the chance to adapt. They're terminated without warning when the company decides they're no longer needed. A friend of mine was terminated on a Sunday — after she gave her team an investor list from one of her clubs.

She was devastated. The sale she had in progress — one I helped to close — went to her team. I received none of the commission.

There are plenty of sharks in this business, so swim deliberately and keep your perimeter in view.

One day, after battling a manufactured issue over a reversal at the end of the month, I heard — deep in my intuition — "You cannot work for a company you cannot trust." Shortly after that, I walked away — leaving a quarter-million-dollar deal on the table. The prospect was a friend of mine. And although I had faith in the retirement product, I had lost faith in both my leadership and my company.

The point I'm making by starting with the Illusion Weaver scenario is this: Your recruiting agent may dress and act like a wealthy man or woman. But agent, beware — know where that wealth is coming from.

That agent will tell you they started where you are. But they will never disclose the manipulation it took to climb higher up the pyramid.

You'll be told you're helping others, but the reality is: others will help themselves off your back, with little return to you.

This first scenario is the most aggressive I encountered — possibly because I stayed there the longest, and lost the most money.

I used nearly $10,000 of my savings to cover mortgage, bills, and sales expenses during that time — in between dry spells and commission reversals. It ended in a fight with unemployment, because the company challenged my filing — even though my claim was made before I ever joined the firm.

Things only got muddier in the months after I left. It wasn't until I encountered the next scenario that I realized this was more of a con game than a mission to serve the community.

The company had added arbitration clauses to its contract, so I couldn't sue in court like agents had over a decade ago.

That's why I'm sharing this. I'm telling you what I wish had been shared with me at the time I was making my decision.

◊ Reality Spark

The contract phase is the most important phase of your hiring process. Read the document line by line — preferably with an employment lawyer.

Realistically, you may not have access to a lawyer. If not, pay close attention to: termination clauses, arbitration language, non-compete, and non-solicitation sections. Know your state's classification of "independent contractor" vs. employee. These clauses can limit your ability to find future work — sometimes by region or even by several years.

In Scenario 3, I encountered a salaried position with a three-year non-compete and a five-year non-piracy clause.

Make sure you count the cost of taking the risk — especially in Scenarios 1 and 2.

Scenario 2: In Community, Not Company, We Trust

"In a consumer society, the community is the true provider of trust, not the market."

— Ivan Illich

Similar to the Illusion Weaver, I found another type of insurance opportunity that deserves a warning. While both types of companies stand on the noble promise of giving agents the chance to help others and better the community, this kind of organization targets a niche group of prospects — giving the illusion that the agent will always have a pool of people to sell to.

What could be better than that? The chance to earn money and serve the community.

What could go wrong?

Several things.

My hope is that I can provide you with enough details so that you'll ask the right questions — and recognize the red flags — when you encounter the "Good Samaritan" recruiter.

First, the prospect group is irresistible to the empathetic salesperson. These are often members of the working class, doing essential jobs for modest wages. You'll admire them — and then find yourself doing similar work, for similar returns.

Your management and support staff will sing praises about agents who "help educate the community," all while helping themselves to large cuts of the money you earn doing so.

I found this pyramid structure even more intimidating than the previous scenario. I lasted only a few months — because I quickly recognized the game.

It was after this experience that I committed to writing this guidance down.

This wasn't your parents' old-school multi-level marketing scam — the kind that makes Amway or vitamin sales look like small fish. These were new-jack sharks, dressed in now in casual clothing.

Recruiters and peers will tell you glowing stories about how people are "making a difference." They'll show up in fancy cars, talk about beach homes and vacations — things you may never see.

For the first two years, you'll just be hoping to stay above water.

In these 100% commission "opportunities", you'll use your own car, your own time, and energy — which you could be investing elsewhere to create a more stable future. They will promise you a mentor, but few people do anything for nothing in return.

I was assigned a mentor who was clearly running a failing business. I was expected to bring in the new clients, the new energy, the new hope. The problem was: I wasn't compensated for the first few months.

The "bonus" I received only covered the cost of doing business. I actually paid more to them than what I was bonused in the first month.

The product wasn't competitive, and the contract was convoluted. The territory was already assigned to a mentoring agent — so we were in competition for leads. He was a nice guy but constantly whining about meeting his numbers and avoiding bonus payback. That alone was a major red flag. But I stayed quiet.

Hands-on training? Nothing like what was promised.

The "flexible schedule"? Subject to my mentor's personal availability — and he didn't always give proper notice.

Many events were over an hour away from my location, and as the days went on, more deception was revealed — through private meetings and double motives.

Of course, the turnover rate was high. And the people who left? Painted as the problem — never the management.

Every story was different, yet the same.

"They didn't follow the rules."

"They couldn't cut it."

"They weren't committed."

Leaders sold themselves as gatekeepers to a "fail-safe" system that would eventually yield returns — but only at the expense of the agent holding up a pyramid of recruiters, brokers, trainers, and trainers to the trainers.

There were a lot of people eating off the agent's plate.

One day, I clicked on my recruiting manager's Outlook profile. There were five people above him with similar titles — everyone a "consultant" or "regional consultant" up the ladder.

No wonder my commission was only 15% on sales.

After taking in so much disappointment from this insurance employment scam, I finally said goodbye. I had seen enough.

I named this section "In Community, Not Company, We Trust" for a reason.

If a corporation has shareholders, then your career development is not the goal — profit is the endgame.

My sales consultant — number one of five— often talked about "low-hanging fruit." Later, I realized the lowest-hanging fruit was us: the agents at the bottom of the food chain.

For every dollar we earned, we gave away 85 cents — with bonus incentives that had to be paid back if sales goals weren't met by the end of the quarter. At least, that's what was supposed to happen to my mentor — who said he was no longer sleeping at night.

So, reader — what should you ask during the interview?

I may sound biased, but I would tell you: avoid this scenario altogether, unless you have:

A pocket full of money

Overflowing energy

A solid side hustle

And gas to burn

But if you're still willing to take the risk, here are some questions worth asking:

◊ Reality Spark

Interview Questions to Ask Before You Sign:

What is the turnover rate of agents in the first year?

What is the average income earned by first-year agents?

Are there any additional expenses I need to consider (e.g., Errors & Omissions, licensing, FINRA registration)? How much will I pay, and when?

What is the company's insurance rating? See if the recruiter knows — but also Google it.

What is my mentor's current profitability in their territory?

How do they receive new prospects?

What is my employment classification — employee or independent contractor?

How will my contract impact my previous unemployment filing if I'm terminated or unprofitable?

May I speak to other agents who have been with the company for more than two years?

Is there a central HR or Compliance Department, or does everything go through the team?

And during the hiring process:

Read all employer and product reviews on career and consumer complaint sites

Look for red-flag language like: "Lack of mentorship ""Favoritism" or "Toxic leadership."

There is no exact science to exposing the illusion. So even if you trust the community you plan to serve, don't put blind trust in the company.

Corporations are not people.

Don't twist your expectations into something the situation doesn't support.

Insurance corporations are well-oiled machines — and they use very little of the empathy they promote during training.

This is Scenario 1 with an empathy twist — but the twist is not for you.

If these two scenarios sound daunting, and you're thinking a hybrid or salaried position might offer more stability — believe it or not, those come with drawbacks too.

Eventually, I'll share the model I found to be the most stable over time.

And I'm open to hearing more stories from agents out there...

But more on that later.

Scenario #3: The Care-Taker

"The sheep will spend its entire life fearing the wolf, only to be eaten by the shepherd."

— Anonymous Proverb

For the agent looking for a little more stability, the next few models might seem like promising opportunities. My experience wasn't ideal, but that doesn't mean yours will be the same. I share this one not to discourage, but to inform—because I was blindsided. I was terminated without warning, and after piecing together the clues, I can't shake the feeling that I had stepped into something far more calculated than it first appeared.

The company was small and independently owned, with most of its business unrelated to property and casualty (P&C). I was hired into what was presented as a growing P&C department at an LLC. Later, I discovered the company operated under several names, one tied to a larger corporation. That only surfaced when I tried to file for unemployment.

The CEO was charismatic and high-energy. She presented herself as a leader who cared deeply about community and well-being. She offered a decent salary, competitive for the insurance industry, and her message checked all the right boxes. I was recruited from a lower-paying role where I had been stuck in a cycle of customer service work under poor leadership. This new firm seemed like a fresh start. It felt like an opportunity to return to sales, learn the ropes, and grow as a licensed advisor.

The branding was strong. The CEO positioned the company as a "caregiver" to the community. She embraced themes of nurturing, spirituality, and purpose. It felt tempting—almost like walking into the gingerbread house from the Hansel and Gretel fairytale.

But beneath that sugary surface, the structure was hollow.

The role I accepted quickly revealed itself to be a façade. Control and manipulation were the true mechanisms of the culture. Employees were expected to perform as loyal caretakers—even martyrs—for the sake of "the mission."

Just one example: lunch breaks were capped at ten minutes. Anything longer had to be scheduled on the shared calendar. While I could have asked for more time if necessary, the culture discouraged any deviation. Micromanagement was repackaged as structure and accountability.

The company appeared to care, but the true loyalty was to profit and perception. Still, I poured myself into the role. I wanted to believe this was the kind of place where I could grow.

The mission included educating clients on every detail of their insurance contracts. Customer service was supposed to be thorough and responsive. In practice, the department was under-resourced. Only one person on the P&C team—the CEO's best friend—was fully licensed to provide customer service. And she was stretched thin.

I was told I would be cross-trained, which made sense in a small firm. I welcomed the learning curve.

I ignored the early red flags, telling myself that no job is perfect. But the signs kept stacking up.

◊ Reality Spark

If something seems too good to be true, it might just be dressed up that way. We're naturally intuitive beings, but our instincts get drowned out when we're overloaded with aesthetics and illusions.

Ask yourself:

> *Why was I hired, and what am I actually being asked to do?*
>
> *Does my experience match the role I've been placed in?*
>
> *Is there a clear training plan, or am I being left to figure things out on my own?*
>
> *Do company leaders communicate with me directly, or only through other staff?*
>
> *Do I feel left out of important conversations or meetings?*
>
> *Are expectations clear during the 90-day probation period?*
>
> *And finally, do leaders walk the talk when nobody else is watching?*

The hiring process moved fast. I had a phone screen, a Zoom interview with leadership, and an in-person visit, all within a few days. I was hired in late spring.

But within weeks, the culture began to feel off.

It reminded me of a cult. New hires were asked to share family photos. There were frequent group icebreakers and one-on-ones to "get to know" each other. Oddly, mine were only with HR. I never had a proper one-on-one with the rest of the team.

Everyone praised the CEO. I found her to be a pleasant, if not particularly exceptional, leader. But I ignored the times I saw her creeping through the halls, eavesdropping. I even overlooked when she brought her large, intimidating dog to the office, like Nino Brown. I welcomed the quirkiness—but the deeper message was clear: power moved quietly and unpredictably.

Most of the employees were related to, personally connected with, or former classmates of the CEO. In hindsight, I wasn't sure what role I was supposed to play in this setup. She was smart, wellness-focused, and progressive, and I even benefited from some of the culture during my early days. Still, the illusion of a supportive workplace was just that—an illusion.

The management team, mostly composed of the CEO's close associates, lacked real experience in insurance or leadership. The P&C department was brand new. Titles and credentials were in place, but actual expertise was scarce.

Still, I didn't question it. I liked the people. I wanted the job to work out. So I ignored the doubts.

I overlooked plenty of things. My benefits wouldn't start until the month of Day 90. The company promised to cover most of the insurance premiums, but with our group size, I suspected the costs would be high—especially for older employees.

I didn't take real lunch breaks, which I now regret. My team was small, and new business wasn't coming in fast enough. Most of our time was spent servicing existing customers—many of them older, tech-averse, and in need of hand-holding.

I valued being supportive, but I was eager to move into an advisory position. Our team lead, though seasoned, was trapped in people-pleasing and visibly overwhelmed. My mentor relied heavily on charm and a frat-boy persona, but the lack of depth eventually became unmistakable.

The company celebrated everything. I didn't mind—it suited my personality—but anything that feels that good needs a second look.

Halfway through my 90-day probation, I started noticing strange things. Someone placed another employee's keys in my bag during a company event. Later, I saw a Microsoft Teams message about them—from the CEO. I wondered if I'd picked them up by accident, but I never got a straight answer.

Employees responded to Teams alerts as early as 6:30 a.m.—well before work hours. The CEO often sent messages during off-hours. After a few months, I stopped reading them until 9 a.m.

A few of my client appointments started disappearing from my calendar. I traced one back to a relative of the CEO. Strangely, it was the president who brought it up in a meeting. I checked the audit trail—and confirmed it had been edited.

At that point, it was obvious. I wasn't being trained for the role I'd been hired for. I was being used for customer service.

There had been no discussion of E&O (Errors and Omissions) coverage. Minimal training in advisory work. Still, I contributed ideas and received positive feedback. On the surface, things looked fine.

But beneath it all, the foundation was cracking.

My mentor began to shift after I professionally pushed back on doing all the customer service work. I wasn't hired to be a full-time CSR.

He began nitpicking, looking for flaws, and trying to intimidate me. I stayed calm until one day I finally said, "If you keep looking for something wrong, you're going to find it."

His training was barely existent. He'd disappear from the office for days—sometimes weeks—always with an excuse.

We did mock customer appointments that felt more like student presentations than training. Eventually, I was reassigned to phone support—second in line behind the CEO's best friend.

There was no real CSR team. Just her—and a part-timer still in school.

Our new phone system tracked every minute of our workday, even bathroom breaks.

During my interview, I'd asked if the job was mostly customer service. I was told, "No—we have people for that."

Apparently, "people" meant 1.5 staffers. And me.

Once everyone on the team, including the CEO, had returned from their summer vacations, I was called into a meeting.

I was terminated.

No review. No explanation. Just: "You're not progressing."

It was Day 91.

◊ Reality Spark

Agent advisors: be cautious of companies that offer just enough sparkle to keep you hanging on.

> ◊ *Ask who's responsible for customer service and how many people are on that team.*
>
> ◊ *Request clarity on the 90-day training process.*
>
> ◊ *Be wary of being hired near summer or holiday seasons—when full-time staff are scarce.*

◊ *If leadership frequently promotes outside services to internal employees, it could be a disguised sales funnel.*

Check online reviews. One red flag might be all you get.

Look closely at your contract. Watch for vague clauses about behavior, image, and post-exit restrictions.

A company that invests more in illusion than infrastructure is likely preparing for turnover—not long-term growth.

This story reads like a fairytale: warm culture, growth potential, paid training, and community-focused messaging. But it ended like a cautionary tale.

If leadership claims to be caretakers, ask what exactly they're taking care of—and at what cost to you.

Salaries are expensive. Health benefits are expensive. Office space is expensive.

But illusion? Illusion is cheap.

This model doesn't earn my trust. Not because it lacked potential—but because it lacked honesty.

For college grads looking for exposure, maybe there's something to gain. But for seasoned professionals, this was a company with unserious management and misplaced priorities.

The choice, as always, is yours.

Scenario # 4 : The Company Man and Woman

To be yourself in a world that is constantly trying to make you something else is the greatest accomplishment."—Ralph Waldo Emerson

Working for a well known brand name in insurance does have its perks. The first is you can negotiate a base salary and commission. Most of these legitimate business owners have been self-sustaining for years, know the business and will be a wealth of knowledge. They do not promise you the pipe dreams as in the other scenarios, but the business models are a little more legitimate. They have access to health brokers and may pay towards your health insurance which can start on Day 1.

So what is the downside? These agents receive commissions directly from the mother insurance company. They are company men and women that build little empires utilizing the popular and well known branding of their organizations. The owners push the brand Liberty Mutual, Allstate, State Farm, Farmers. Overhead can make or break their bottom lines, so you might find yourself working in environments with limited amenities such as heat, air and bathroom facilities shared by everyone in the office.

My experience was with an owner that was top of his agent class, but he micromanaged, provided an uncomfortable atmosphere to work in for half of the team. We were chained to the telephones and every minute was preplanned. I was promised that I would have access to his book of business, but I was assigned the outdated contacts and other coworkers would sometimes steal my customers callbacks and commission. Since everyone was a veteran agent, I had no real argument so I worked under the conditions for as long as I could. If I needed personal time, I was docked in pay which was a very low base with a draw that I needed to exceed, in order to see my commissions.

I made several contacts and sold several policies, but I rarely saw above $20 extra in commissions in a paycheck. I asked to move from full time to part time, as I had work life balance needs at home, so he dropped my rate per hour. Other coworkers were allowed to work hybrid and take care of life, but I was too new he said to do the same. After a year, I believe he would have considered providing me more flexibility. I could not last more than seven months putting out that amount of energy for such little pay. A guy that looked like he was right out of college was hired after me.

I believe these sort of jobs are best fit for people that do not have the responsibilities of children or aging parents that require time and care off of the standard 9-5:30p schedule. I believe with the proper environmental controls and paid time off, I might have stayed a little longer. I guess I am just not a Company person.

In the end, this was the scenario I chose out of all four options. It felt the most grounded — a structured environment with a reputable brand and a clear, proven business model. There were no grand promises or illusions, which was a relief compared to what I experienced in the other scenarios.

That said, it still wasn't an ideal fit. The lack of flexibility, inconsistent peer support, and limited pay made it hard to justify long-term. I don't regret giving it a shot, but it reinforced the importance of knowing what kind of work culture I can truly thrive in.

For those who value structure and can adapt to a traditional agency model, this may be a solid stepping stone — just make sure the environment aligns with your real-world needs, not just your professional goals.

Note: These scenarios were not experienced in consecutive order but rather at different stages of my journey in the industry.

What I didn't realize then was that even after leaving one of these companies, the complications don't always end. Sometimes, they follow you long after your last day — especially when it comes to unemployment compensation.

Unemployment Compensation Nightmare

Lastly, the reader should know: the 100% commission scenarios often lead to nightmares for those filing unemployment claims. In both of my commission-based experiences, I was already receiving unemployment and had to attend hearings just to resume the benefits I had before I ever met the sweet-talking salesman or saleswoman.

Agent beware — these companies can be retaliatory, unfair, and unscrupulous. It doesn't matter whether you take unemployment during your time with them, claim it as an independent contractor, or not at all. Many will still drag you before the unemployment magistrate without warning.

Not only are you left picking up the financial and emotional pieces of your life, but you may also be forced to sit through appeals, potentially pay back overpayments, or face delays depending on the unemployment rules of your state.

Without proper perspective, this can result in even greater loss of time, energy, and peace of mind long after the partnership has ended.

Before signing any contract, know that there is often far more going on behind the scenes than you're led to believe. Many of these corporations and mutual insurance companies have arbitration systems designed to sidestep accountability and avoid class-action lawsuits.

Even Scenario 3 delayed my unemployment compensation by refusing to provide feedback on why I was terminated. I live in an "at-will" employment state, and they took advantage of every loophole in the system — even the loopholes have loopholes.

If you're not industry-savvy, there is a strong possibility you are entering an illusion disguised as opportunity — not something designed to stabilize your career or help you grow.

While all organizations are not created equal, I hope this publication has given you fuel to dodge the illusions of modern-day Ponzi schemes and snake oil sales disguised as entrepreneurship.

A Final Word to Insurance Agency Owners

If you're an agency owner and find yourself offended by this material, I challenge you to add your voice to the conversation. We wnt to hear from those who do it right — because your presence is needed more than ever.

I personally would appreciate hearing about your business model. You have the power to challenge harmful practices in your industry, especially if you remember where you started — as an agent, just like the rest of us.

Your leadership is needed to restore integrity, inspire confidence, and attract and retain talented professionals who genuinely want to serve clients and build careers in this field.

And to the Agents...

To the agents: *they need us*. These companies cannot function without the feet on the ground.

It is only in numbers that we can begin to transform exploitative business practices in our industry. And one of the most powerful tools we have is our stories.

So I invite you to share yours — whether disappointing or hopeful — so that we can reshape the current culture into something more ethical, more empowering, and more sustainable. Let's keep the conversation going.

✉ Send your feedback to:

qowblazinglight@gmail.com

"Just because you swim with sharks doesn't mean you have to be part of their school."

— Q.O.W

Don't miss out!

Visit the website below and you can sign up to receive emails whenever Q.O.W publishes a new book. There's no charge and no obligation.

https://books2read.com/r/B-A-UUEEF-AFOXI

BOOKS 2 READ

Connecting independent readers to independent writers.

www.ingramcontent.com/pod-product-compliance
Lightning Source LLC
LaVergne TN
LVHW101618210926
848480LV00009B/821